GIANT KILLERS

GIANT KILLERS

PERSONAL STUDY GUIDE

ANGI JEFFCOAT

Copyright © 2023 Angi Jeffcoat

All rights reserved. No part of this book may be reproduced or used in any manner without the prior written permission of the copyright owner, except for the use of brief quotations in a book review.

To request permissions, contact the author at info@angijeffcoat.com.

Unless otherwise indicated, all Scripture quotations are taken from the *Holy Bible*, New Living Translation, copyright © 1996, 2004, 2015 by Tyndale House Foundation. Used by permission of Tyndale House Publishers, Inc., Carol Stream, Illinois 60188. All rights reserved.

Scripture quotations marked NIV are taken from THE HOLY BIBLE, NEW INTERNATIONAL VERSION®, NIV® Copyright © 1973, 1978, 1984, 2011 by Biblica, Inc.® Used by permission. All rights reserved worldwide.

Scripture quotations marked ESV are taken from The Holy Bible, English Standard Version®. Text Edition: 2016. Copyright © 2001 by Crossway, a publishing ministry of Good News Publishers. The ® text has been reproduced in cooperation with and by permission of Good News Publishers. Unauthorized reproduction of this publication is prohibited. All rights reserved.

Scripture quotations marked NKJV are taken from the New King James Version®. Copyright © 1982 by Thomas Nelson. Used by permission. All rights reserved.

Personal Study Guide ISBN: 979-8-9898664-4-1
Library of Congress Control Number: 2024901684

Cover and book design by Allison East

TABLE OF CONTENTS

CHAPTER 1
Giant Killer: Overcoming Fear 13

CHAPTER 2
Confidence Reclaimer: Overcoming Low Self-Image 19

CHAPTER 3
Ground Shaker: Overcoming Discouragement 25

CHAPTER 4
Culture Defier: Overcoming Toxic Culture 31

CHAPTER 5
Joy Restorer: Overcoming Shame 37

CHAPTER 6
Sea Crosser: Overcoming the Trauma of Your Past 43

CHAPTER 7
Peace Speaker: Overcoming Anxiety 49

CHAPTER 8
Wall Destroyer: Overcoming Rejection 55

CHAPTER 9
Debt Forgiver: Overcoming Bitterness 61

CHAPTER 10
Divide Reconciler: Overcoming Self-Focus 67

CHAPTER 11
Wave Walker: Overcoming Doubt 73

CHAPTER 12
Legacy Leaver: Overcoming an Orphan Spirit 79

A NOTE TO THE READER

This personal study guide is designed to help you process, both internally and externally within a group setting, the content you are reading in Giant Killers. You will get out of this what you put into it. I encourage you to be completely honest with yourself and ruthlessly transparent with your small group each week. That is the only way to receive freedom and healing in these areas of your life. James 5:16 says to "Confess your sins to each other and pray for each other so that you may be healed." The reality is this: You need the people in your small group. *There is healing for you in the confession and transparency.*

You can do this. Don't let the enemy tell you otherwise. Let's dive in together and begin killing giants!

All my best,

Angi

A NOTE TO THE SMALL GROUP LEADER

The Giant Killers Personal Study Guide is designed as a tool for individuals to process what they've read in the book Giant Killers, both internally and externally within a small group setting. Each chapter of the study guide coincides with the chapter they will read in the book. Individuals can write in this study guide and are encouraged to write a personal declaration at the end of each week's study.

WHAT YOU CAN EXPECT
You will find the same layout in each chapter of the study guide so that you experience consistency and ease in this process.

OPEN IT UP!
This section will contain a couple of light-hearted questions to get people talking (and maybe even laughing!) as your group members are still arriving. There will be an opening prayer prompt here as well.

TO SUMMARIZE...
This section will introduce the giant for that chapter and give a short synopsis.

DISCUSS
This section contains two questions that address the subject on a broad level. You are encouraged, for the sake of time, to choose one question to discuss.

READ THE OPENING PASSAGE AS A GROUP
You'll find a prompt to read the opening passage for the chapter to familiarize everyone with the Bible story that chapter is based on.

PROCESS TOGETHER

In this section, each main point of the chapter is broken down into three discussion questions. This is designed to go deeper with the material. As the leader, I want to encourage you to lead the way in vulnerability and transparency! Challenge group members to be honest with themselves and to trust the group with their answers. You most likely will not have enough time to cover every question. There should be more than enough content for you to work with. Do not be afraid of awkward silences! Out of those pauses, the introverts in your group will muster the courage to speak up and share what is in their heart.

CLOSING PRAYER
This section includes content-relevant prompts to praise, repent, ask, and yield to God.

BETWEEN SESSIONS
This section contains suggestions for writing a personal declaration and reading it out loud during the week. This might be a new concept for people, so I would like to encourage you as the leader to walk them through it and normalize it for them.

On the first week, you'll want to set aside a little extra time to introduce the concept of personal declarations. Have one written in advance that you can share as an example. On week two, have a couple of people read their declarations from week one out loud. Also, there is a journal prompt in this section. Some people process well through journaling. This section is *not for everyone!* Think of it as a "bonus" section specifically for those who enjoy processing on paper.

Thank you for walking with your group through this process. Thank you for having a heart to pour into others. Thank you for creating a safe space for people. Now, it's time to kill some giants!

All my best,

Angi Jeffcoat

CHAPTER 1

Giant Killer: Overcoming Fear

TRUTH: "I AM EQUIPPED"

OPEN IT UP!

→ Has anyone gotten your name wrong before, such as on your coffee order or a teacher in school? What are some funny things you've been called?

→ Are there hurtful names you have been called throughout your life (stupid, dummy, airhead, a mistake, etc.)?

→ As you open the group in prayer, let's release the pain of any hurtful names and memories to the Lord. Let's invite Him throughout this study to heal our hearts and help us to reclaim the identity Christ gave us.

TO SUMMARIZE...

Fear is one of the largest giants of our day, but God has given His children the power to defeat it.

The giant of Fear blinds us from noticing how God has prepared us to face the challenges that come our way. It works to convince us that we

CHAPTER 1

are not enough—capable enough, strong enough, smart enough, likable enough, blessed enough—to overcome the things that plague us with fear. Fear can keep us trapped and stagnant, unable to walk into the rooms and do the things necessary to fulfill our purpose and calling. Together, let us process how your experiences have prepared you to be ready to act counterculturally and to show up with winning tools so that we can step into our identity of Giant Killer.

FEAR IS ONE OF THE LARGEST GIANTS OF OUR DAY, BUT GOD HAS GIVEN HIS CHILDREN THE POWER TO DEFEAT IT.

DISCUSS
Choose one of the following questions to discuss:

- → Can you think of a moment when you were overcome with fear?

- → What is your greatest fear?

READ THE OPENING PASSAGE AS A GROUP.

- → 1 Samuel 17:3-51

PROCESS TOGETHER

RECOGNIZE HOW YOUR EXPERIENCES HAVE PREPARED YOU:

- → What does it look like to be present where God has you currently? What are you learning in this season?

→ What are some past experiences in your life that God used to prepare you for your current challenge?

→ Has God spoken to you about the specific calling of your life? Maybe you are skilled at starting businesses, or you are gifted in working with children. Maybe God has given you the gift of leading people or a desire to do mission work. If you are unclear about your calling, do not worry! God has a plan for your life! Read Jeremiah 29:11, and ask God to show you His calling for your life.

BE READY TO ACT COUNTERCULTURALLY:

→ Can you think of a time when you were paralyzed by fear or confusion? If you are willing, share it with the group. What circumstances led you to this state?

→ Have you ever been swept up in drama at work or with your family? How did you break free from the drama?

→ In 1 Samuel 17:8, Goliath accuses God's army of being "only the servants of Saul." He reduces them to their job title. Do you find your identity in what you do? How can that be limiting for you? List some of your identities beyond your job title, such as father, friend, sister, leader, connector, peace-maker, etc.

> "You are more than your circumstances; you are more than a role or a title."

SHOW UP WITH WINNING TOOLS:

→ David was tempted to wear Saul's armor as a false sense of security. Is there anything in your life currently that can create a

CHAPTER 1

false sense of security for you? In the time of prayer at the end, let's confess that to God and declare that you will not lean on a false sense of security any longer.

→ Insecurity can lead to fear. In times when you have struggled with insecurity, how did that feed into fear?

→ Choose a verse from the Scriptural support section of chapter 1 that could help you the next time you struggle with the giant of Fear. Share that verse with your group.

> "You can't win the battle if you aren't willing to step out onto the field."

CLOSING PRAYER:

→ **PRAISE GOD** that you are no longer enslaved to Fear. Thank Him for giving you all you need to be a Giant Killer.

→ **REPENT** of times when you have surrendered to Fear or a false sense of security.

→ **ASK** Him to help you reclaim this identity of Giant Killer. Ask the Holy Spirit to set you free from any fearful mindsets or lies of the enemy that you have believed about yourself.

→ **YIELD** to whatever God speaks to you or asks you to do. This will produce great fruit in your life.

BETWEEN SESSIONS:

→ **WRITE YOUR DECLARATION** for Giant Killer based on what you highlighted or what stood out to you. Read it out loud, daily if possible. Are there aspects of these statements that you are still struggling with? Pray specifically about those parts and invite the Holy Spirit to help you.

→ JOURNAL: Write down a verse that stands out to you from the Scriptural support section. Write a couple of sentences as to why this jumps out at you. Write a short prayer asking God to help you apply this verse to your daily life.

MY GIANT KILLER DECLARATION:

FOR NEXT WEEK:
Read Chapter 2 of *Giant Killers*.

CHAPTER 2

CHAPTER 2

Confidence Reclaimer: Overcoming Low Self-Image

TRUTH: "I AM ANOINTED"

OPEN IT UP!

→ Is there a quirky thing about yourself that you find funny? How would your roommate or spouse answer that question?

→ If you had to describe yourself in three words, what would they be?

→ Can you relate to having an inner voice that criticizes your words and actions? What does this voice sound like?

→ As you open in prayer, invite the Holy Spirit to reveal to you times when you have listened to a negative inner voice rather than the truth of what He says about you. Pray for restoration in your view of yourself.

CHAPTER 2

TO SUMMARIZE...

We often build our self-image on the wrong foundation. We listen to negative self-talk. We get discouraged when we depend on self-reliance, only to let ourselves down. Sometimes, we even grasp for the temporary approval of others through people-pleasing. These pitfalls can cause our self-image to plummet. Satan loves it when we fall into these traps! He comes alongside us when we are feeling low to speak lies to us about our identity. He attempts to show us false proof through our circumstances. Let's dig into these temptations so we can steer clear of them and build our self-image based on who God says we are.

DISCUSS

Choose one of the following questions to discuss:

→ Have you ever struggled with a low self-image? How did this perception control your response to opportunities, relationships, etc.?

→ How does the way others describe you differ from how you see yourself?

READ THE OPENING PASSAGE AS A GROUP.

→ Judges 6-8

Note to the Leader: This is a longer opening passage. Choose some key verses from it in advance, and have group members read those verses to save time for conversation.

PROCESS TOGETHER

REPLACE NEGATIVE SELF-TALK:

→ Judges 6:15 shows us examples of how Gideon was speaking curses over himself. Have you unintentionally spoken curses or negativity over yourself? Can you pinpoint a time when this led to a self-fulfilling prophecy?

→ Are you gracious toward others but critical and judgmental of yourself? Where do you think this harsh self-talk comes from? If you continue to listen to this negative self-talk over time, how do you think this will impact your life? Your job? Your relationships?

→ Choose a verse from the scriptural support section of chapter 2 that speaks the truth of how God sees you. Plug your name into it and read it out loud.

THIS IS A CALL TO EVERY OUTCAST, EVERY PERSON WHO FEELS LESS THAN OR NOT ENOUGH. GOD SEES YOU AS MORE!

ELIMINATE SELF-RELIANCE:

→ How is God's view of self-reliance vastly different from people's view of self-reliance?

→ Why do you think God doesn't want us to rely solely on ourselves and our own strength?

CHAPTER 2

- → We see in 2 Corinthians 12:9 that in our weakness God's strength is made perfect. What does that look like in our everyday life? Can you give an example?

> "God will not share the throne of your heart with your flesh."

AIM TO PLEASE GOD, NOT PEOPLE:

- → Can you think of a time when you had to take a stand for something that was unpopular? What were the consequences? Do you believe that God was pleased by your actions?

- → Do you struggle with people-pleasing? When are you especially tempted by this? (example: when your job depends on it, when it comes to your family, etc.)

- → How can people-pleasing be dangerous to your self-image? If your focus was only to please God, how could that bring stability to your self-image?

> "The quickest way to lose your anointing is through people-pleasing."

CLOSING PRAYER:

- → PRAISE GOD for how He sees you. Thank Him for always seeing more in you than you see in yourself.

- → REPENT of any harsh or hurtful self-talk. Repent of any desire to please other people instead of God.

- → ASK God to show you how He sees you. Ask Him to reveal negative self-talk that you didn't notice existed.

- → YIELD any areas of your life that you are trying to accomplish in your own strength. Invite His strength so that He can receive all glory!

BETWEEN SESSIONS:

- → WRITE YOUR DECLARATION for Confidence Reclaimer based on what you highlighted or what stood out to you. Incorporate as much Scripture as possible to rewire some of your previous views of yourself. Read your declaration out loud and boldly! Declare the truth that "I am anointed."

- → JOURNAL: Write down a verse that stands out to you from the Scriptural support section. Write a couple of sentences as to why this jumps out at you. Write a short prayer asking God to help you apply this verse to your daily life.

MY CONFIDENCE RECLAIMER DECLARATION:

_____
_____
_____
_____
_____
_____
_____
_____

FOR NEXT WEEK:
Read Chapter 3 of *Giant Killers*.

CHAPTER 3

CHAPTER 3

Ground Shaker: Overcoming Discouragement

TRUTH: "I AM SET FREE"

OPEN IT UP!

→ This chapter opens with an embarrassing car story. Do you have a funny or embarrassing car story?

→ Can you think of an answered prayer or blessing that you would like to PRAISE GOD for?

→ Do you have a prayer request, something that is weighing heavily on your heart and mind? As you open in prayer, release the highs and lows of your week to God. Invite Him to come and speak to any discouragement that you might be experiencing.

TO SUMMARIZE...

Our praise touches the heart of God. When we praise Him in the midst of our pain or exhaustion, He is especially moved. He inhabits the praises of His people (Psalm 22:3). That verse means that His presence fills our praise. As we praise God, it takes our focus off our circumstances and places it on His power and character. Through praise, the world around us may not change, but the world within us does. Let's process how praising God in our situation is the solution that can lead to a powerful shift in our hearts—a shift that will help us reclaim the identity of Ground Shaker.

DISCUSS
Choose one of the following questions to discuss:

→ Describe one of the most discouraging times of your life. What circumstances caused the discouragement? How did you cope with these feelings?

→ Describe your state of mind when you are discouraged. How does it affect your performance at work or relationships with those close to you?

READ THE OPENING PASSAGE AS A GROUP.

→ Acts 16:16-40

PROCESS TOGETHER

RELEASE UNMET EXPECTATIONS:

→ Exhaustion can lead to discouragement. Are you feeling exhausted in this season of your life? Read Matthew 11:28-30 in The Message. What does Jesus tell us to do when we are feeling weary or exhausted?

- → What are some unmet expectations in your life that are clouding your mind with discouragement? What would it look like to release those to God and be free of that burden?

- → Paul had just recruited Silas and could easily have blamed himself for getting them both imprisoned. This would have been a false sense of blame that would have only increased his feelings of discouragement. Are you taking on a false sense of blame for your circumstances? How could God be using these situations for His glory?

ONLY WHEN YOU RELEASE UNMET EXPECTATIONS ARE YOUR HANDS OPEN TO RECEIVE THE PROMISES AND PLANS GOD HAS FOR YOUR LIFE.

SHIFT THE ATMOSPHERE:

- → What opportunities to praise God where He's never been praised before can you identify in your day-to-day life?

- → Paul and Silas worshiped through their pain. For them, that looked like singing praise in the darkest moment. What does it look like for you to worship through your pain?

- → One of the best solutions for discouragement is getting your focus off your circumstances and placing it on God's power, strength, and goodness. Choose a verse from the scriptural support section that proclaims God's power and character and read it aloud.

CHAPTER 3

> "Praise Him in places where He's never been praised before."

SET OTHERS FREE:

- → Paul and Silas led the other prisoners with praise. How can you lead those around you (family, friends, neighbors, co-workers) with praise?

- → Paul and Silas praised God not only for their freedom but also for the freedom of those around them. Whose freedom could your praise impact? Is there someone in your life whom you would like to see set free?

- → Praise causes a shift in the atmosphere of our lives. Where do you need the atmosphere to shift? At home? At work? In your heart or mind?

> "We need to praise God when it doesn't make sense to praise Him!"

CLOSING PRAYER:

- → PRAISE GOD for His strength and power. Praise Him for His goodness and faithfulness.

- → REPENT of taking on a false sense of blame for your circumstances. Repent of keeping your eyes on your circumstances and not on Him.

- → ASK the Holy Spirit to show you moments when you need to put on the garment of praise.

GROUND SHAKER: OVERCOMING DISCOURAGEMENT

→ YIELD both the circumstances and the outcome to Him. Then praise Him despite it all!

BETWEEN SESSIONS:

→ WRITE YOUR DECLARATION for Ground Shaker based on what you highlighted and what stood out to you in this chapter. Include as much Scripture as possible to take your focus off your circumstances and onto His power and character. Read it out loud as often as possible to fill the atmosphere with praise and to help you reclaim your identity of Ground Shaker.

→ JOURNAL: Find three or four verses in the book of Psalms that declare the praise of God. Write them in your journal along with a short prayer of praise (in your own words) to God.

MY GROUND SHAKER DECLARATION:

_____
_____
_____
_____
_____
_____
_____
_____
_____
_____

FOR NEXT WEEK:
Read Chapter 4 of *Giant Killers*.

CHAPTER 4

Culture Defier: Overcoming Toxic Culture

TRUTH: "I AM SET APART"

OPEN IT UP!

→ This chapter talks about a good type of defiance, one that goes against the destructive ways of the world around us. Did you ever have a rebellious phase as a kid? Describe it to those around you.

→ Do you find it difficult to stand up for what you believe is right? As you open in prayer, ask God to reveal how and when to defy the culture around you and to give you a holy boldness to do so.

TO SUMMARIZE...

While we are on this earth, God is calling us to be Culture Defiers, to rebel against the norms and accepted "truths" of this world, to passionately revolt against standards and expectations placed on us by those who do not fear God, to live by a standard that is otherworldly, and to do what

CHAPTER 4

doesn't make sense to those around us. As we begin by defying a culture of Busy, a culture of Self, and a culture of Hate, we will find that there is a better, higher way that awaits us.

DISCUSS

Choose one of the following questions to discuss:

- → Can you think of a time when you were surrounded by a toxic culture? Describe what made it toxic.

- → Do you feel like you are easily swayed or impacted by the culture around you? Explain your answer.

READ THE OPENING PASSAGE AS A GROUP.

- → Luke 10:25-37

WE OFTEN USE THE BUSYNESS OF OUR LIVES TO COVER UP BROKENNESS. WHAT STARTS OUT AS A BADGE OF HONOR QUICKLY BECOMES A MASK TO HIDE OUR PAIN AND DYSFUNCTION...OFTEN FROM OURSELVES!

PROCESS TOGETHER

DEFY A CULTURE OF BUSY:

→ Sometimes we keep ourselves moving to avoid the pain of our past. Is there pain from your past or a current tension that you are trying to mask with activity? Pause and ask God to show you what is in your heart.

→ Do you struggle with people-pleasing or feeling the need to say "yes" to everything? What do you think is the root cause?

→ What are two to three areas where you could say "no" or eliminate commitments to create margin?

RESIST A CULTURE OF SELF:

→ Would you consider yourself to be somewhat selfless, always tending to the needs of those around you, or would you admit that your life is mostly centered around you? Would those closest to you agree with your answer?

→ Do you often feel the need to prove yourself, to climb to the top at any expense in your career? Read Matthew 20:16. Describe practical ways that you could approach your life/career differently through the lens of this paradigm shift.

→ Do you feel a burning need for justice to come to those who have wronged you? Are you always the one with the final word or the last laugh? Read Matthew 5:44. How does Scripture tell us to treat our enemies?

CHAPTER 4

COMBAT A CULTURE OF HATE:

- → What if you were the Samaritan in this scenario? Would you be able to defy everything in your nature, everything from your culture, to sacrifice for this person who might still hate you?

- → Before we can help people who have been overlooked by society, we need to determine who those groups of people are in our community. What are some of the groups of people who are marginalized or overlooked in your community? (ex: homeless, elderly, disabled, etc.)

- → What are some practical ways you can overcome barriers to engage with people who have been overlooked by society?

> "...we have to engage with people in a way that defies cultural expectations and helps people who have been overlooked by society."

CLOSING PRAYER:

- → PRAISE GOD because His ways are higher than our ways. He provides a better way for us to walk through life.

- → REPENT of selfish thinking and for making things all about you. Repent of not actively engaging with people who have been overlooked or marginalized.

- → ASK for guidance of how or when to speak up or do something. Pray for boldness to step out into something countercultural.

- → YIELD your schedule to God. Invite Him to heal any brokenness that you might be trying to cover up with Busy.

CULTURE DEFIER: OVERCOMING TOXIC CULTURE

BETWEEN SESSIONS:

→ WRITE YOUR DECLARATION for Culture Defier based on the work of freedom from Self or Busy or Hate that the Holy Spirit does in your heart. Some of your declaration will be by faith, meaning it may not be what you see coming out of you right now, but this is what you are trusting God to do within you. Use Scripture from the scriptural support section and anything that jumped out at you from the chapter.

→ JOURNAL: What area of your life is God challenging with the paradigm shift of Kingdom thinking right now? Write a few sentences about what you sense the Holy Spirit speaking to you in this area. Write an action step that you need to take in this area. Then write a short prayer asking God to help you to grow in this process.

MY CULTURE DEFIER DECLARATION:

_____
_____
_____
_____
_____
_____
_____
_____
_____
_____

FOR NEXT WEEK:
Read Chapter 5 of *Giant Killers*.

CHAPTER 5

Joy Restorer: Overcoming Shame

TRUTH: "I AM REDEEMED"

OPEN IT UP!

→ What was a high and a low from your week?

→ As you open in prayer, ask the Holy Spirit to reveal areas where you wrestle with Shame. Ask Him to give you boldness to share openly today and to be healed.

TO SUMMARIZE...

The giant of Shame stalks about, attacking people with small sins and large ones alike. Even the nicest, purest people can fall prey to this evil giant. He hides around corners and waits for the moment when we mess up to spew his venomous whispers. Once Shame has his talons in you, he influences you to suppress your emotions, only to make room for more shame. He persuades you to withdraw from being vulnerable, to close relationships, and to avoid healthy community so that his voice is the dominant one in your mind. He feeds into feelings of depression,

CHAPTER 5

anxiety, and worthlessness. He even prevents you from taking healthy risks. We will overcome the giant of Shame today by challenging his labels, resisting the urge to shrink under his weight, and reflecting on God's redemption.

DISCUSS

Choose one of the following questions to discuss:

→ Do you relate to any of these characteristics? If so, which ones?

- Do you believe that you do not measure up?
- Do you think that you are unworthy to serve in ministry?
- Do you correct things you say in conversations and frequently feel you have to "fix" what you say?
- Do you wrestle with constant insecurity?
- Do you feel like you often make dumb mistakes or say embarrassing things?
- Do you struggle with the same sin over and over, even after you repent?

→ Can you pinpoint a time or event during your past in which you began struggling with the giant of Shame?

READ THE OPENING PASSAGE AS A GROUP.

→ Luke 15:11-32

PROCESS TOGETHER

CHALLENGE SHAME'S LABELS:

→ What are some labels that have been placed on your life, either by yourself or others?

→ The Prodigal Son was going to ask to be brought on as a hired servant in his father's house because he didn't think he deserved to be treated as a son after all he had done. Can you relate to this feeling? Have you ever treated yourself as a servant rather than as a son or daughter in God's house?

→ The father in this story challenged Shame's label of servant by declaring the correct label of "son." What are some correct labels that God speaks over your life that will challenge Shame's labels?

> **OUR HEAVENLY FATHER REFUSES TO ENTERTAIN THE THOUGHT OF HIS SONS AND DAUGHTERS TAKING ON A LESSER ROLE IN HIS KINGDOM.**

RESIST THE URGE TO SHRINK UNDER SHAME'S WEIGHT:

→ Was there a time in your life when you struggled with hopelessness? How did you overcome it?

→ Read Jeremiah 29:11. How does this verse infuse you with hope?

CHAPTER 5

- → In the story, the father exceeded the son's hopes. Can you think of a time in your life when God exceeded your hopes or prayers?

> "When the weight of Shame becomes unbearable, your Father's arms are there to catch you!"

REFLECT ON GOD'S REDEMPTION:

- → In this story, the father runs to the son as he is coming home. Why are you grateful that we serve a God who runs to us in our Shame?

- → Can you think of a time when you have experienced the mercy of God (a time when you didn't receive the punishment you deserved)? Share that with the group.

- → James 5:16 says to "Confess your sins to each other and pray for each other so that you may be healed." We do not confess our sins to each other for forgiveness. God has already forgiven us. We confess to our brothers and sisters in Christ so that our hearts can be healed from secrets and shame. If you are struggling with the giant of Shame in your life, would you be so bold as to confess it? Allow the group to surround you with grace and love and to pray for your healing.

CLOSING PRAYER:

- → PRAISE GOD for His love and mercy! Thank Him for being a good Father who runs to us when we've messed up.

→ REPENT of receiving the labels of Shame. Thank God for exposing the lies of Shame and for declaring your true label of son or daughter!

→ ASK God to reveal any lingering lies of Shame in your heart or mind.

→ YIELD any desire to treat yourself as "less than" in God's Kingdom. Receive the mercy and love that He pours out over you today!

BETWEEN SESSIONS:

→ WRITE YOUR DECLARATION for Joy Restorer. Fill it with as much Scripture as possible from the scriptural support section. Use victory statements such as, "Fear not; I will no longer live in shame." Include the truth that "I am redeemed." Read your declaration out loud, daily if possible.

→ JOURNAL: Write new identities that God has lovingly placed on your life based on the truth of Scripture. In His word, God declares that you are more than a conqueror, victorious, loving, generous, righteous, etc. Exploring these identities instead of the ones Shame tries to place on you will begin to restore joy in your heart.

MY JOY RESTORER DECLARATION:

_____
_____
_____
_____
_____
_____
_____
_____
_____
_____
_____
_____
_____

FOR NEXT WEEK:
Read Chapter 6 of *Giant Killers*.

CHAPTER 6

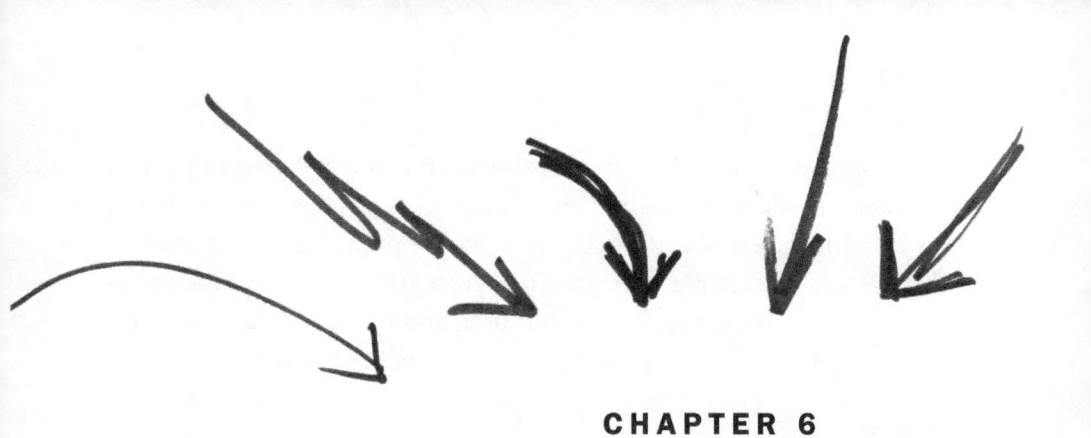

Sea Crosser: Overcoming the Trauma of Your Past

TRUTH: "I AM MADE NEW"

OPEN IT UP!

→ What is the craziest thing you did as a child or teenager that made your mom nervous (had she known)?

→ Describe how you've changed since receiving salvation. What differences in you would those closest to you identify?

→ As you open in prayer, thank God for setting you free from sin and transforming your heart. Thank Him for Jesus' blood, through which you have "become a new person. The old life is gone; a new life has begun!" (2 Corinthians 5:17)

TO SUMMARIZE...

God called the Israelites out of Egypt, out of a life of slavery and oppression. He had something much better in store. However, they did not go from slavery directly into the Promised Land. They had to cross through

CHAPTER 6

the desert first. They did not go from victim to conqueror overnight. There was a wilderness journey in between. Often in our lives, we do not go from the slavery of our past directly into the promises of God. We find that there is a desert place we must first cross. This is because God forms our character, closes the door on our past, and walks with us. Let's leave our past behind us as we explore our identity of Sea Crosser.

DISCUSS
Choose one of the following questions to discuss:

→ Has God already brought some healing to your heart from past trauma? How did that healing impact your current relationships and outlook?

→ Share your salvation story with the group. Celebrate God's grace and goodness to rescue you from sin and bondage.

READ THE OPENING PASSAGE AS A GROUP.

→ Exodus 14:13-31

PROCESS TOGETHER

WITH GOD, NOTHING IS WASTED.

WITNESS HOW GOD FORMS YOUR CHARACTER:

→ Can you relate to feeling stuck in the desert, the in-between place? Do you feel that God has placed a dream for your future in your heart but hasn't opened the doors for it yet? Try to identify and verbalize some ways God is strengthening your character during this time.

→ Is there something that happened to you in your past that you had no control over and that you had to overcome? How did you refrain from taking on a victim mentality?

→ Can you think of an inner vow that you have made to yourself? What have the unintended consequences been?

> "Being healed of pain does not mean that the wrongs never occurred. It just means that they will no longer define or control you!"

WATCH HOW GOD CLOSES THE DOOR ON YOUR PAST:

→ How have you seen God's power at work in your life?

→ In what area(s) of your life today do you need God to show His power?

→ Read 1 Corinthians 15:57. What does this mean for your life today? What does this mean for your emotional healing?

RECOGNIZE THAT GOD WALKS WITH YOU:

→ In the Bible, we see that God would walk with Adam and Eve in the cool of the day. Walking in the garden was their special time together. Do you have a special time set aside to be with God?

CHAPTER 6

- → Has God walked with you through a dark time in your life? Describe that time and God's faithfulness *through it*.

- → Are you in a difficult season right now? If so, share with the group, and take a moment to pray with one another.

"GOD WALKS CLOSELY WITH US THROUGH DIFFICULTY, DEATH AND DESERTS."

CLOSING PRAYER:

- → PRAISE GOD because He is powerful! Thank Him for being a good Father who wants to walk with us.

- → REPENT of a victim mentality. Thank God for healing you from past wounds and declare that today is your day of freedom!

- → ASK God to reveal and heal any wrong ways of thinking that are lingering from your past.

- → YIELD any inner vows to God. Recognize that He is your Protector, and He holds your life in His hands.

BETWEEN SESSIONS:

- → WRITE YOUR DECLARATION for Sea Crosser. Fill it with as much Scripture as possible from the scriptural support section or from the chapter. Use victory statements such as, "I have been given victory over sin and death through our Lord

Jesus Christ" (1 Corinthians 15:57). Read your declaration out loud, daily if possible.

→ **JOURNAL:** Romans 6:6 says that you are no longer a slave to your sin. If you want the visual representation, write down some words to describe you in the past and cross them out with a black marker. Then write some words to describe the transformation work that the Holy Spirit has done within you. Thank God for delivering you from your past, once and for all.

MY SEA CROSSER DECLARATION:

FOR NEXT WEEK:
Read Chapter 7 of *Giant Killers*.

CHAPTER 7

Peace Speaker: Overcoming Anxiety

TRUTH: "I AM SECURE"

OPEN IT UP!

- → Describe the worst physical storm you have ever experienced. Where were you?

- → How did you find safety? How did God protect you through that storm?

- → As you open in prayer, thank God for having the power over the storms of life. Pray that the Holy Spirit will reveal and heal any areas of anxiety in your heart.

TO SUMMARIZE...

Jesus is and has always been the Prince of Peace, the Ruler of Peace. Before time as we know it began, before He created the very sea the disciples were sailing in, He was the Prince of Peace. This is His nature, and He has given us authority in His name to be Peace Speakers as well (John

CHAPTER 7

14:12). For us to reclaim our Christ-given identity of Peace Speaker, we must see how in Mark 4, the name of Jesus enables us to face storms with God's power, confront challenges in the light of God's presence, and stand strong in trials with God's promises. This will encourage you! Not only is the original Peace Speaker in your boat with you . . . He has empowered you to speak to the wind and the waves!

DISCUSS
Choose one of the following questions to discuss:

- → Is anxiety something you struggle with? If so, what typically triggers it?

- → What are some ways you have attempted to mitigate anxiety in the past?

READ THE OPENING PASSAGE AS A GROUP.

- → Mark 4:35-41

PROCESS TOGETHER

FACE STORMS WITH GOD'S POWER:

- → Are you currently going through an internal storm in your life? If so, what "waves" do you need Jesus to calm?

- → What would it look like for you to go through this storm in life with total peace? What impact would that have on you personally? (Example: "I would sleep better." Or "I wouldn't snap at my kids.")

- → Ephesians 6:12 tells us that our battle is in the spiritual realm, although it often feels like it is with a person. In what relationship do you need to be a Peace Speaker?

> **"THE ATTACK IS STRONGEST WHEN GOD IS ABOUT TO DO SOMETHING SIGNIFICANT."**

CONFRONT CHALLENGES IN THE LIGHT OF GOD'S PRESENCE:

- → Once you recognize that this particular storm is a spiritual attack, what are some action steps you can take to address it head-on and position yourself to speak peace? (Example: pray for the other person, humbly apologize, turn on worship music, etc.)

- → What aspects of your current stressors are beyond your control? What would it look like for you to release them to Christ?

- → Read Isaiah 26:3. How can you maintain peace of mind until you are through this storm?

STAND STRONG IN TRIALS WITH GOD'S PROMISES:

- → Read Philippians 4:6-7. What does this passage mean to you? What does it look like in your everyday life?

- → Verse 7 refers to a peace that transcends or goes beyond all human understanding. How can this apply to your current situations that are causing anxiety?

CHAPTER 7

→ In what ways does the storm inside you match the storm around you? What steps should you take to address this before you can become a Peace Speaker to others?

> "We need to be Peace Speakers to our own hearts before we can be Peace Speakers to our families and the people we encounter in our daily lives."

CLOSING PRAYER:

→ **PRAISE GOD** for having all power over the storms of life. Worship Him as the Prince of Peace.

→ **REPENT** of your attempts to control the circumstances of your life instead of casting your cares at His feet.

→ **ASK** the Prince of Peace to do a supernatural work of peace within your heart so you can become a Peace Speaker in your home and work.

→ **YIELD** your heart and situation completely to Christ and His care.

BETWEEN SESSIONS:

→ **WRITE YOUR DECLARATION** for Peace Speaker based on what you highlighted and what stood out to you in the chapter. Fill it with as much Scripture as possible from the scriptural support section. As you read your declaration out loud, choose the Scripture that is speaking to you the most to meditate on and think about throughout your week.

PEACE SPEAKER: OVERCOMING ANXIETY

→ JOURNAL: In Isaiah 9:6, we see that God is our Wonderful Counselor, Mighty God, Everlasting Father, and the Prince of Peace. If you are at a crossroads and need to make a decision, write a short prayer to the Wonderful Counselor. If you are in a difficult situation and need a miracle, write a short prayer to Him as Mighty God. If you need forgiveness and affirmation, call upon the Everlasting Father in your prayer. If you are struggling with anxiety, write a prayer to the Prince of Peace.

MY PEACE SPEAKER DECLARATION:

FOR NEXT WEEK:
Read Chapter 8 of *Giant Killers*.

CHAPTER 8

Wall Destroyer: Overcoming Rejection

TRUTH: "I AM LOVED AND PURSUED"

OPEN IT UP!

→ Can you think of a time when you felt the most loved? Describe that time to the group and why you felt loved.

→ What can you do in this group to help those around you feel safe and accepted?

→ As you open in prayer, ask the Holy Spirit to gently reveal any areas of rejection in your heart or past so that they can be healed.

TO SUMMARIZE...

The giant of Rejection can keep us hidden and isolated, keeping ourselves from experiencing the love and community God has for us. Rejection can sneak into our hearts when we do not realize it is there. We are so quick to move on with our lives and not "dwell in the past" that

CHAPTER 8

we miss the wound that a rejection encounter can leave on our hearts. We see in John 4, however, that Jesus is not okay with the fear of rejection ruling our decisions. He is not okay with past wounds eating at us in secret. He loves us too much to let us remain as we are. He lovingly encourages us to destroy our walls so we can rest in the reality that He meets us where we are, understands that He calls us out of hiding, and tells others of Jesus' love. Let's dive into this together and discover how we can become Wall Destroyers.

DISCUSS

Choose one of the following questions to discuss:

→ Describe a moment in your life when you felt rejection.

→ How has the pain of rejection impacted your relationships?

READ THE OPENING PASSAGE AS A GROUP.

→ John 4:4-42

PROCESS TOGETHER

REST IN THE REALITY THAT JESUS MEETS YOU WHERE YOU ARE:

→ One of the names of God is *El-roi*, which means *"the God who sees me."* What does this tell us about His character and heart? How does knowing this about God bring comfort to you?

→ There are two common approaches to dealing with rejection: pulling away from close relationships out of fear of rejection and rejecting others before they can reject us. Do you identify with one of these unhealthy rejection responses? If so, which one? Can you give an example?

→ How do you know that you are carrying the pain of rejection? The woman at the well hid from others to avoid further rejection. Is there an area of your life where you are hiding to avoid further rejection?

> "He sees our rejected hearts and does not sit passively on a throne in the distance."

UNDERSTAND THAT JESUS CALLS YOU OUT OF HIDING:

→ Have you ever tried to ignore the pain of rejection? How did that impact you over time?

→ Read Ephesians 1:6 in the NKJV. What do you think it means to be "accepted in the Beloved?"

→ Why do you think Jesus calls us out of hiding? Why did He call the woman with the issue of blood out in front of everyone in Luke 8:47?

> "YOU MIGHT BE ABLE TO HIDE YOUR REJECTION AND PAIN FROM YOURSELF, BUT YOU CANNOT HIDE IT FROM HIM."

CHAPTER 8

TELL OTHERS OF JESUS' LOVE:

→ Have you come from a religious background that taught you that if you sinned or made a mistake, God would reject you? Choose a verse from the Scriptural support section that shows us the opposite. Read it out loud.

→ Jesus knows what it is like to forgive those who rejected Him. Is there anyone in your life who made you feel rejected who you need to forgive? What action steps can you take to forgive them?

→ Revelation 12:11 says that we overcome by two things: the blood of the Lamb and our testimony. How can sharing your testimony of freedom from Rejection help to set others free from the giant of Rejection?

> "If Jesus rejected you,
> He would not have gone to the cross for you!"

CLOSING PRAYER:

→ **PRAISE GOD** for being *El-roi, the God who sees you.* Thank Him for loving you too much to leave the pain of Rejection lingering in your heart.

→ **REPENT** of believing any lies of the enemy that you are rejected by God. Repent of any times you have rejected others, intentionally or unintentionally.

→ **ASK** God to heal any wounds from Rejection in your heart and make you whole.

→ YIELD your heart to Jesus by forgiving and releasing anyone who has rejected you.

BETWEEN SESSIONS:

→ WRITE YOUR DECLARATION of Wall Destroyer based on what stood out to you in the chapter. Fill it with Scriptures to rewire any past thinking that God rejects you when you mess up. Read your declaration out loud and daily if possible.

→ JOURNAL: We cannot control Rejection from others, but we can be confident in our identity of Wall Destroyer. Find two Scriptures about the unconditional love of God from the scriptural support section and write them in your journal. Write a short prayer of thanks for the unconditional love and acceptance of God.

MY WALL DESTROYER DECLARATION:

_____
_____
_____
_____
_____
_____
_____
_____
_____
_____
_____

FOR NEXT WEEK:
Read Chapter 9 of *Giant Killers*.

CHAPTER 9

Debt Forgiver: Overcoming Bitterness

TRUTH: "I AM FORGIVEN"

OPEN IT UP!

→ Did you ever get into a fight as a child? Did you reconcile when it was over? If so, what did that look like?

→ Forgiveness is a painful and difficult subject for many. As you open in prayer, invite the Holy Spirit to give you strength to be honest with yourself and to address any unforgiveness in your heart.

TO SUMMARIZE...

Anytime we allow unforgiveness to linger unaddressed in our hearts, it invites the giant of Bitterness to enter our lives. In Matthew 18, Jesus shares a sobering parable warning us of the consequences of unforgiveness. This is powerful motivation for us to examine our hearts closely to see if there is any unforgiveness or Bitterness hiding there. It's time to release the hold of

CHAPTER 9

Bitterness, let go of entitlement, and pursue reconciliation so we can overcome the giant of Bitterness and step into our identity of Debt Forgiver.

DISCUSS

Choose one of the following questions to discuss:

- → If you're brutally honest, have you struggled with forgiving those who have wronged you?

- → What has previously held you back from forgiving those who have hurt you?

READ THE OPENING PASSAGE AS A GROUP.

- → Matthew 18:21-35

PROCESS TOGETHER

RELEASE THE HOLD OF BITTERNESS:

- → Have you been in a relationship where you felt like a doormat being stepped on? If it's not too painful, describe it. How would you handle that relationship differently as a Debt Forgiver?

- → Have you withheld forgiveness because you didn't think the person deserved to be forgiven? How has that affected you more than him/her?

- → Have you ever thought you forgave someone but later realized you had not? Describe how you knew you hadn't forgiven them. Knowing now that forgiveness is an ongoing thing, what should you do the next time you feel that way?

> **"WE THINK WE'RE PUNISHING OUR OFFENDERS BY NOT FORGIVING THEM, WHEN WE REALLY ARE ONLY PUNISHING OURSELVES."**

LET GO OF ENTITLEMENT:

- → Is there someone in your life who you need to forgive? What is one specific way you can pray for them?

- → Judgment is reserved for God alone. When someone hurts us, the injustice stirs within us a desire to judge them. Search your heart. Is there judgment that you need to repent of?

- → When this person wronged you, it created a wound. How can you invite God into this wound so that He can help you heal?

PURSUE RECONCILIATION WITH OTHERS:

- → What is the key difference between forgiveness and reconciliation?

- → Is there someone who you need to reconcile with? Refer to the four steps to pursue reconciliation in this chapter. Have you attempted any of these steps?

- → Are you holding an offense toward anyone? If you are holding onto hurts, it is time to forgive. It is never easy, but we are called to live in peace with those around us as far as it depends

CHAPTER 9

on us (Romans 12:18). Ask your group to pray for you that God would help you to forgive.

> "One-sided reconciliation is abuse."

CLOSING PRAYER:

→ PRAISE GOD for forgiving a debt we could not pay. He led the way in being a Debt Forgiver!

→ REPENT of holding on to Bitterness or judgment.

→ ASK God to heal the wound that this person caused. Ask God for supernatural strength to truly forgive.

→ YIELD any desire or perceived right to hold on to offenses.

BETWEEN SESSIONS:

→ WRITE YOUR DECLARATION of Debt Forgiver based on what stood out to you in this chapter and on the Word of God from the scriptural support section. Read it out loud. Even if you do not feel like a Debt Forgiver yet, begin declaring that you release those who have hurt you and you will not be a prisoner to Bitterness any longer!

→ JOURNAL: If you are struggling with forgiving someone, write a letter to them in your journal. Be very honest about what they did to hurt you. Then write that you release them from this offense, that you forgive them. Then, if you can, write a short prayer of blessing over their life. This letter is not to give to them. It is to help you process internally and let go of offense. It will help you to move forward with a healed heart.

MY DEBT FORGIVER DECLARATION:

FOR NEXT WEEK:
Read Chapter 10 of *Giant Killers*.

CHAPTER 10

Divide Reconciler: Overcoming Self-Focus

TRUTH: "I AM CALLED"

OPEN IT UP!

→ Was there someone in your life who prayed for you to receive salvation? Are you here today because of their prayers?

→ Who are you praying for to receive salvation?

→ As you open in prayer, ask God to give you a passion, a holy burden, to pray for the lost.

TO SUMMARIZE...

Intercession is for all followers of Christ. When we intercede in prayer, we are assailing Heaven with petitions for someone. We are reconciling the divide between God and His people. We are attempting to urge God to move on behalf of another. God is calling us to stand in the gap through prayer for those He has placed in our lives. The habit or lifestyle of intercession is a good one to have because we often need to get our

CHAPTER 10

focus off ourselves and onto others. Let's explore this identity of Divide Reconciler and what it means to stand in the gap, be an armor-bearer, and honor your leaders.

DISCUSS
Choose one of the following questions to discuss:

- → Who is the most selfless person you know? Describe how they are selfless.

- → Do you often catch yourself making things all about you? How do you think that impacts the people around you?

READ THE OPENING PASSAGE AS A GROUP.

- → Numbers 16:41-50

PROCESS TOGETHER

STAND IN THE GAP:

- → Moses and Aaron were fighting for the very lives of the people who revolted against them and attacked their leadership. Sometimes, the people who are the most horrible to you are the very ones who need prayer. Can you think of a person in your life who hurt you but needs your prayers?

- → In a practical sense, what does it look like to forfeit any right to offense?

DIVIDE RECONCILER: OVERCOMING SELF-FOCUS

→ Are you willing to walk with people as a Divide Reconciler even when it is inconvenient? Can you think of a time when someone else did this for you?

> "For a Divide Reconciler, stepping into the mess of people's lives requires that you forfeit any right to offense."

BE AN ARMOR-BEARER:

→ The devil is strategizing against your family and loved ones. We need to deploy ourselves to go to war through prayer on behalf of others. Make a list of those you need to intercede for:

→ Read Ephesians 6:13-17. Process as a group what it looks like to pray each piece of the armor of God over your loved ones. Make notes of anything that stands out to you:

→ What do you do when you don't know how to specifically pray for others? Read Romans 8:26. Who is there to help us and to reveal how to pray?

CHAPTER 10

> "Make no mistake. This is war! And it is won on your knees."

HONOR YOUR LEADERS:

→ Have you ever served under a leader who you didn't like? Whether it was poor leadership or just a difference of opinion, God calls us to honor leadership. How can you still be honoring to leaders who are wrong or unfair?

→ Have you ever coveted someone else's position of leadership? What are some practical ways to honor that person and remain content where God has placed you?

→ One of the best ways to honor leaders is to earnestly pray for them. What specific leaders has God placed in your life who you need to pray for?

CLOSING PRAYER:

→ PRAISE GOD for those He placed in your life to intercede for you, including Jesus!

→ REPENT of not praying for your loved ones often.

→ ASK God to show you who to interced for. Ask the Holy Spirit to show you how specifically to pray.

→ YIELD any selfish desires or self-focus to God and ask Him to make you a Divide Reconciler.

BETWEEN SESSIONS:

→ **WRITE YOUR DECLARATION** of Divide Reconciler based on what stood out to you in this chapter and on the Word of God from the scriptural support section. Read it out loud. Declare that you are a Divide Reconciler, and your prayers are powerful and effective! (James 5:16)

→ **JOURNAL:** Write a short prayer for a different person each day this week. (Some prayers will come easier than others.) This will be a practical way to help you develop the muscles of intercession.

MY DIVIDE RECONCILER DECLARATION:

FOR NEXT WEEK:
Read Chapter 11 of *Giant Killers*.

CHAPTER 11

Wave Walker: Overcoming Doubt

TRUTH: "I AM SAVED BY GRACE"

OPEN IT UP!

→ Have you ever witnessed a miracle? If so, share it with the group to build up faith.

→ Do you have a prayer request for you or a loved one?

→ As you open in prayer, praise God for the miraculous ways He has moved in the past. Then offer up the current prayer requests to God, inviting Him to do the impossible once again.

TO SUMMARIZE...

As Wave Walkers, we are called to overcome doubt and impossibilities. However, there is a difference between limitations and impossibilities. Limitations are opportunities to trust God's sovereign plan for our lives; impossibilities are opportunities to step out in faith. Jesus desires to do the impossible, the miraculous in your life. Jesus calls us to walk on the

CHAPTER 11

water with Him. As we reclaim this identity of Wave Walker, let's look at how Jesus is calling us to step out of comfort zones, redefine success and failure, and walk by faith and not sight.

DISCUSS

Choose one of the following questions to discuss:

- → Describe a situation in your life that felt impossible.

- → Identify some limitations in your life. How do you see the grace of God through some of these limitations?

READ THE OPENING PASSAGE AS A GROUP.

- → Matthew 14:22-33

PROCESS TOGETHER

STEP OUT OF YOUR COMFORT ZONE:

- → How is God calling you to leave the familiar in your life? Where is He calling you to step out of your boat and into the unknown?

- → What are some ways that you might be too attached to your comfort zone to be willing to step out into what God is calling you to?

- → Are there people in your life who cheer you on or give you confidence to step out by faith?

> "Jesus will invite you to go where you never thought possible."

REDEFINE SUCCESS AND FAILURE:

→ If you attempt to step out of your boat and into the unknown in your life, what is the worst that could happen? If the worst did happen, how do you think Jesus would respond?

→ Even though it might be painful, think back to some of your moments of perceived failure. Are you measuring failure/success of those events through the world's lens of success, through your personal expectations, or through a Kingdom perspective?

→ If Jesus is truly our only hope, what does it look like to invite Him into your situation?

> "Failure is not a lack of success; failure is a lack of effort."

WALK BY FAITH AND NOT BY SIGHT:

→ What does "walking by faith" look like today?

→ Can you think of a time when you had to trust God's voice and not what you saw in the environment around you?

→ What are some areas in your life where you want Jesus to do the impossible? Where do you need a miracle?

CHAPTER 11

> "LIMITATIONS ARE OPPORTUNITIES TO TRUST IN GOD'S SOVEREIGN PLAN FOR OUR LIVES; IMPOSSIBILITIES ARE OPPORTUNITIES TO STEP OUT IN FAITH."

CLOSING PRAYER:

- → **PRAISE GOD** for being the God of the impossible! Praise God that what is impossible with man is possible with Him!

- → **REPENT** of trusting in what you can see around you instead of trusting in God.

- → **ASK** Him to strengthen your faith and help you to have the courage to get out of the boat. Ask Him to help you discern the difference between limitations and opportunities to step out in faith.

- → **YIELD** the outcome to Him. Declare by faith that He can rescue you or resurrect you!

BETWEEN SESSIONS:

- → **WRITE YOUR DECLARATION** of Wave Walker based on what the Holy Spirit was speaking to you through this chapter. Fill your words with Scripture from the scriptural support section. God's Word will redefine failure for you and increase your faith so you can walk with confidence. Read your declaration out loud and with boldness!

→ **JOURNAL:** Read 2 Corinthians 4:18. In your journal, list some things that are seen that you have looked to in the past for security, such as a job or money or your strengths and abilities. Write a short prayer to Jesus, telling Him that you will no longer trust in these things. You will trust in Him as you step out of the boat.

MY WAVE WALKER DECLARATION:

FOR NEXT WEEK:
Read Chapter 12 of *Giant Killers*.

CHAPTER 12

Legacy Leaver: Overcoming an Orphan Spirit

TRUTH: "I AM ADOPTED AS
A CHILD OF GOD"

OPEN IT UP!

→ Describe the legacy your parents are passing down or have passed down to you.

→ What characteristics have your parents passed down to you that you want to pass down to your children or impress on those close to you?

→ As you open in prayer, invite the Holy Spirit to search your heart and show you if there are pains from your past that are unaddressed.

TO SUMMARIZE...

People think legacy is about death, but it is much more about how you live your life. That means you shouldn't wait until you are at death's door

CHAPTER 12

to establish legacy. This identity is for everyone in Christ—single, married, children, no children, rich or poor, young and old alike. The reality is that you are leaving behind a legacy—good, bad, or otherwise—whether you realize it or not. This realization makes it vital to invest time in building a spiritually rich, virtuous one. As we explore what it means to be a Legacy Leaver, you will discover ways to conform to God's image, take back ground from the enemy, and open up to community. Let's invite God to speak to us as we reclaim this identity!

DISCUSS
Choose one of the following questions to discuss:

→ What do you want to be known for when you die?

→ If you had to write out what was going on your tombstone when you die, what would it say?

READ THE OPENING PASSAGE AS A GROUP.

→ Acts 9:1-20

PROCESS TOGETHER

CONFORM TO GOD'S IMAGE:

→ Look back to the list of 10 Traits of an Orphan Spirit Leader. Are there any of these traits that you struggle with?

→ What symptoms of an orphan spirit do you identify in some of your relationships?

LEGACY LEAVER: OVERCOMING AN ORPHAN SPIRIT

→ Knowing that you are adopted into the family of God and are now a son or daughter, how does that change your approach to your career? How does it change your approach to God? How does it change your relationships with others?

"AN ORPHAN SPIRIT IS WHEN CHRIST FOLLOWERS CLAIM TO KNOW GOD AS A LOVING FATHER BUT INWARDLY BLAME HIM FOR PAST PAIN AND REJECTION."

TAKE BACK GROUND FROM THE ENEMY:

→ Read 2 Corinthians 2:11 and 1 Peter 5:8. What "runs in your family" that could actually be the enemy's scheme against your legacy? (ex: alcoholism, adultery, abandonment, etc.)

→ Can you identify lies of the enemy that you struggle to overcome? Write them below and share them with the group to bring the light of Jesus into this area of your heart.

_____
_____
_____

→ Perhaps one of the greatest legacies you can leave is one of a heart that has been healed and restored. As a group, take a minute or two to reflect in silence. Ask the Holy Spirit to show you a moment from your past that needs to be healed. If you would be so bold, share this with the group and receive prayer.

CHAPTER 12

> "You need to be healed before your legacy can heal the generations to come."

OPEN UP TO COMMUNITY:

→ Like Saul, did you have a moment when God got your attention that changed everything? If so, share it with the group. This was your moment of spiritual adoption! Do you relate to the scales falling off his eyes?

→ How can you lean more on your church family? What practical steps can you take to open up to community? (You're already off to a great start by being a part of this group!)

→ Read Romans 8:15-17. What does it mean that you are not only a child of God but also an heir of God? How does that impact your legacy?

> "As children of God, we are called to be interdependent with one another, not independent of each other."

CLOSING PRAYER:

→ PRAISE GOD that He is a good and loving Father. Thank Him for adopting you into His family.

→ REPENT of any lies that you have unknowingly believed about God's character.

→ ASK the Holy Spirit to continue to show you any places in your heart that need to be healed. Ask Him to show you how you can better open up to community.

- → YIELD your legacy to God. Invite Him to continue to show you what *He wants it to be.*

BETWEEN SESSIONS:

- → WRITE YOUR DECLARATION of Legacy Leaver based on what you highlighted and what the Holy Spirit is revealing. Declare that you are a new creation and that your adoption is sealed! Fill your declaration with Scripture, and boldly read it out loud when you are finished.

- → JOURNAL: Write some observations from this chapter. What stood out to you? Are there conversations you need to have that you are dreading? Write a prayer asking God to help you with this. With extreme honesty, invite Him into the brokenness that you feel. Watch as He meets you with grace and compassion in this process!

MY LEGACY LEAVER DECLARATION:

THANK YOU FOR GOING ON THIS JOURNEY WITH US OF RECLAIMING OUR IDENTITY AND STEPPING OUT AS GIANT KILLERS!